Basics of Poultry Farm

1. Farm history and future planning

Poultry breeding has always been an integral part of the livestock system in India. Bird production in India has taken a qualifying leap in the last four decades, with the production of a commercial production system from a completely unorganized and non-scientific farming system with ultra-modern technology interference. The Indian commercial poultry sector has made great progress due to the scientific adoption adopted by the industry and due to a government-made environment. The Indian poultry sector is generally divided into organized and incompatible sub regions. Requirements for each sub-sector are very different. The Government of India has met the needs of each sub-sector for the development of poultry development programs and industrialists. Central poultry development organizations are playing an important role in coordinating and propagating these development programs of the government.

1.1 Farm history

- **Regional poultry farm** :-

  The origin of Central Poultry Development Organizations (CPDO) in Chandigarh, Bhubaneswar and Mumbai, Central Poultry Development Institute and Training Institute, Bangalore and Central Poultry Performance Testing Center, Gurgaon.

  Central Poultry Breeding Farm, Chandigarh

  This organization was initially established by the Punjab Government for this institution

  After the reorganization of the state of Punjab in 1.11.1966, this organization came under the name of Chandigarh Administration's County Project, Chandigarh. It was further brought forward on 1.4.1978 after the administrative control of the administration of Chandigarh by the Ministry of Agriculture, and it was named central poultry breeding farm, Chandigarh.

1 Infrastructure Planning

The demand for modern poultry infrastructure in India is in line with the increase in the size of poultry farms. In the first poultry farm there were a few hundred birds (200-500 poultry) production per cycle. However, at present, poultry units with less than 5000 birds are an exception, with a majority of more than 500,000 bird-bearing farms. Similarly, the rectilinear is similar in the fields of the chickens.

The Indian poultry equipment market estimates hundreds of crores and estimates of annual growth rate of 10 percent. Another important reason for the poultry machinery industry is the rapid growth of poultry processing industry. With the increasing demand of quality poultry products, it has become very important to adopt good machinery to ensure the quality of Indian Poultry Units. Most basic equipment such as hatchers / incubators, feeders, poultry houses, even environmental-controlled and pre-fabricator houses etc. are indigenous products.

2.1 The basic principles of poultry farming

- The state's position and design will follow the state pollution control board.
- The farm will not be retained at least 100 meters from any major drinking water source and 500 meters from any other animal / poultry farm industry.
- The farm should be fenced up to a height of 8 feet with fencing / concrete boundary fence, which would provide suitable safe entry and outlet.
- The field will be widened with a green belt and at least two rows will not be more than 3 meters.
- Proper drainage / outlet will be provided for accumulation and discharge of storm discharge / waste

discharge (possible to detect the theory of rainwater harvesting).

- No barrier will be made for any water course in the field or beyond the boundary of the farm.

2.2 Basic Principles of Poultry Housing

- It should be located on a highly raised and properly maintained site.
- The long axis of the house had to face east-west direction, to avoid direct sunlight in those areas which experienced energy and drafts in the majority of last year. If the farm is in the cold field then the long axis to be north-south.
- The length depends on the number, type of bird and the nurturing method. The width not exceeding 9 meters or 30 feet to prevent the collection of ammonia in the shed.

3.0 Simple management

Poultry production is very dynamic as institutional and management changes. In today's business environment, there is rapid growth of appropriate capacity as per the changing system. Although stability often requires dependence on other fields such as feed / compact input and processing facilities. In India, the growth rate of the poultry sector can be due to many factors, such as rising income and a rapidly expanding middle class, as well as the consumption of poultry producers by reducing production and marketing costs by rising consumer prices Have diminished concrete production, changes in the market of cold and fertile products from living birds, and policies that ensure the supply of competing fish and soybeans. In future, the key to the growth of poultry industry in India. In addition, monitoring, monitoring and control of the disease will also decide the fate of this area. Contemporary, India's unorganized and yard poultry sector is one of the most powerful tools for creating landless / marginal farming industries and providing nutritious security to rural poor.

3.1 Preparation of the shed before boarding

- Spray the insecticide after the removal of old birds.
- Remove all non-stationary equipment and the remaining feed toys and containers.
- Eliminate all rodents and wild birds if any.
- Remove all compost, garbage, feathers, doves, dust, and any other organic material by cracking hard brush.
- Remove all the weeds and rubbish from outside the house, burn feathers, etc.
- Remove the wire / feathers from wire mesh, cheese, cracks, cage and floor using fire guns.

4. Breeds

The definition of races varies and is widely debated. Largely we adopt the following version:

(A) Sub-special group of domestic animals or birds which are defined by the identified and known external symptoms, which can be separated by visual variation from those other similarly defined groups within the species; Or

(B) A group for which its separate identity has been accepted due to geographical and / or cultural differences from similar groups.

JERSEY GIANT

NEW HAMPSHIRE

PLYMOUTH ROCK

RHODE ISLAND RED

BRAHMA

COCHIN

(Source of breeds images,6 ; Instructional Materials Service Texas A&M University)

5. Reproductive management

5.1 Reproductive Plans

5.1.2 Occupational and time consuming scientific reproduction

There is a never ending search for reproduction. Depending on the success of any reproduction program, the natural change in birds is exploited so that the chosen stock can be properly selected for crossing. It takes about eight years, racially selects and develops new genetic lines, so that it can be tested in a variety of situations and can be started as a new commercial product.

5.2 Glossary of reproduction

- The basic stock that produces the hybrid, when crossed with another line or race. Produces pure line and stock, grandparents and parents' qualities when confused by a scheme.
- Grad's parents are actually pure line birds, but they can not be used to produce a pure line or grandparents, they can produce parents only.
- Parents can produce only commercial hybrids in a special combination with another line or race.
- A stock can not be physically identified; Grandparent, parents, commercial utilization is limited to the economic age of the birds and should be prepared from the stock of the pre-era generation.

6 Nutrition and food

Converting poultry to food and foods in food products is the result of high nutritional requirements for their high rates of productivity. Poultry requires at least 38 nutritional wires in their houses which have adequate density and balance. After a comprehensive review of statistics, the minimum nutritional requirements of poultry are available from the level of experience. The criteria used to determine the requirements for the given substance include increased growth, feed efficiency, egg production, prevention of deficiency symptoms and the quality of poultry products. These requirements assume that nutrients are in bioplast form, and they do not include a limit on safety. Consequently, different feed stones should be adjusted based on the biopsy of nutrients. Combine a difference of safety on the basis of changes in the rate of food consumption due to environmental temperature or dietary energy, genetic stress, adherence conditions (especially the level of hygiene) and the presence of stress and diseases including microboxins.

7 Feed form

- Mash Feed: Grated and mixed with raw materials. It is usually feeds, easy to prepare and economical
- Petit Feed: Prepared by exposing mash feed to heat for treatment under pressure. In the amounts of heat and bacteria, anti-nutritive factors are added in heat, which enables feed for better capitalization. This system of feed reduces feed brunt
- Caramels : The cane is divided into scripts. Compared to mash and knot, feed preparation is very expensive.

8 Poultry Health and Disease Diagnostics

Animal health and human health are interlinked - Over the centuries, germs that cause disease in humans arise from domestic or wild animals. In addition, both animals and humans are affected, and are influenced by their environment. Genocotos can be transmitted to humans through food, direct contact between animals and humans, or through other routes. An unprecedented increase in the movement of people and people around the world, environmental, forest deforestation, environmental change and transformation, urbanization, animal protein such as milk, eggs and meat, economic development, and international pet petals. Businesses are just a few factors that have given greater opportunities for animal transmission and transmigration of germs among humans.

The OIE wants to strengthen the activities for the purpose of resolving the "one health" concept: It works in partnership with other world organizations to prevent, control and eliminate the diseases present in animals, humans, and the interstitial interfaces. So it is important to have a strategy that focuses on animal resources at low levels; Early warning; Rapid Confirmation of Doubtful People; Quick Reply; And fast and transparent notifications It is important to have a manual that describes the optimal diagnostic method for diagnosing the disease by describing internationally approved laboratory diagnostic techniques.

Poultry injections are widely applied to prevent and control contaminated poultry diseases. The purpose of their use in the production of poultry is to increase or decrease the elimination of the clinical disease at the agricultural level, thereby increasing the production. Vaccines and vaccination programs are broadly different in relation to many local factors (such as the type of product, local pattern of infection, cost and potential damage) and are generally managed by the poultry industry. In the last decade, due to poultry's major epidemic diseases (avian influenza and new-castle disease), financial deficits have become heavier both for commercial and public sectors. In this way, vaccination should also be made in the structure of the program of eradication of poultry disease at national or regional level under public supervision of public veterinary services.

9 Vaccination in poultry

Immunization is a vaccine of antigen specific antioxidants to promote resistance or resistance against diseases.

- Types of Vaccine
  -Live vaccinations
  -Naturally, with micro-organisms yielded or retired with Attenuated Stories.

10 Diseases, Visual Guides in Poultry

10.1 bacterial diseases

- Escherichia coli - Escherichia coli infections are divided into poultry of all ages and categories. They primarily belong to poor health-conditions, treated technical needs or sensitive and immunosuppressive diseases. A typical sequence of novella infections is local or extended peritonitis.

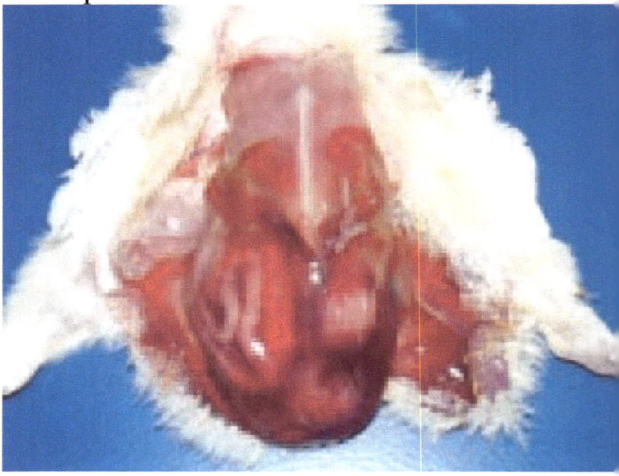

- Fowl cholera- A common herd among the adult flock spread through the filth, feed and water, elegant erect ruff feathers with swollen, difficult to breathe.

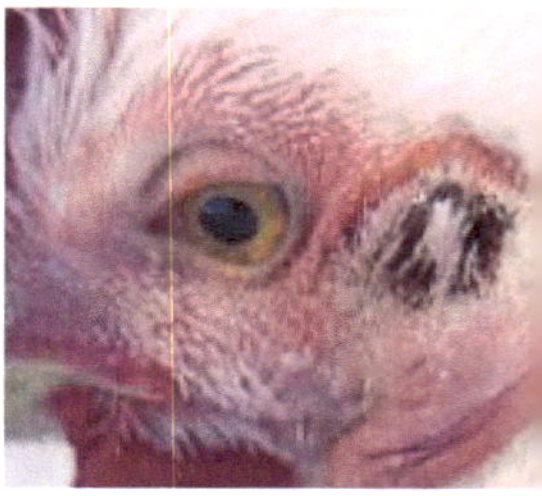

- Botulism - Botulism is addictive toxic substances of clostridium botulinum. With the exception of the vultures, most birds are sensitive. Clinical signs stop for several days within a few hours. Paralysis is seen in the absence of legs, feathers, neck and eyes. rapidly making paralysis progressive and birds fall into a deep coma with embrace and are usually carried forward. There are no solid lesions. Treatment with Selenium, Vitamin A, D and E, as well as some antibiotics such as Chlortetracycline, bacterin etc. may reduce the mortality rate.

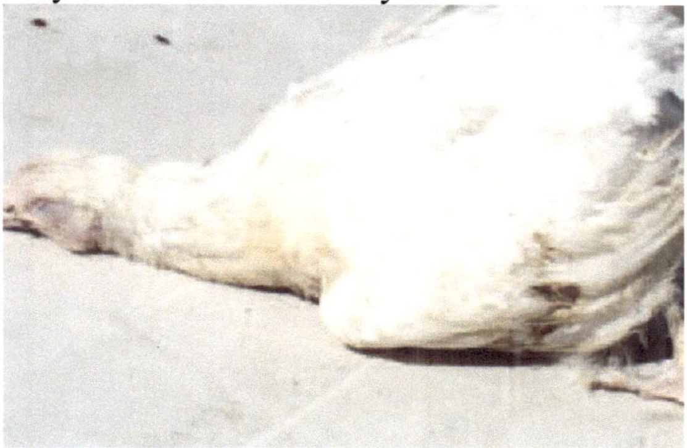

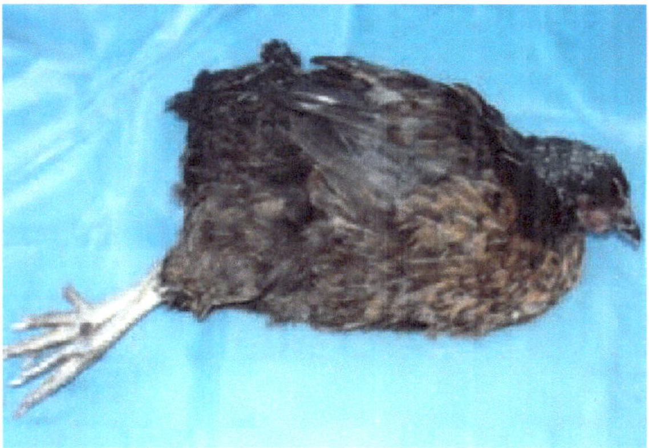

- Mycoplasma respiratory symptoms and prolonged illness lasting longer. Especially at all ages hens and turkeys are. Auto biological Agent M. Galileoptm But in many cases, the jurisdiction has been promoted because it belongs to any or all of its agents: Koli, P. Maloxida, H. Paraglinarum and IB or ND Virus The most common symptoms of adult flocks are to reduce the production of signs, rash, cough, cough, egg production. In more than 4 weeks, more and more diseases occur in polar crumbs during the winter and the disease course is more serious and in the case of related infections. Often, conjunctivitis, facial skin umbilical cord and wipes may be exposed.

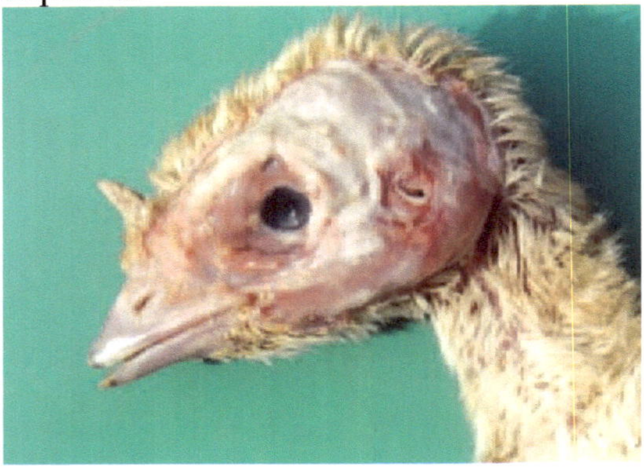

- Avian TB is a serious contagious disease that involves the formation of granulomatous lesions, a progressive weight loss and death. This is usually found in birds gathered in small yards, there is a problem among the zoo and the worshipers of foreign birds.

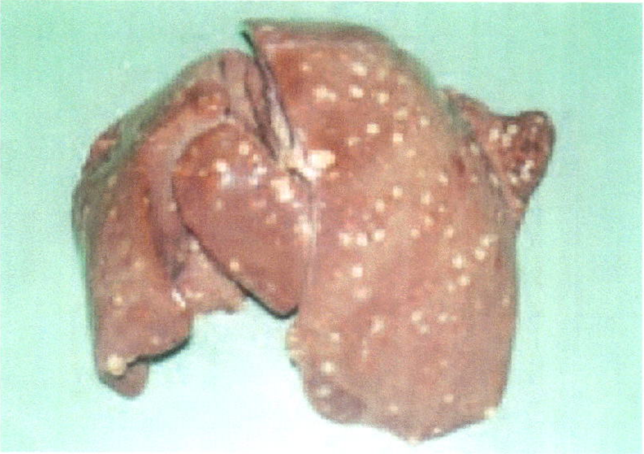

- Gangrene Dermatitis (GD) is a disease that affects the fat and growing birds, including clotting of different skin areas and severe cellulitis of the upper tissues of the skin. The sudden and rapid increase in mortality rate is the first gesture for the growth of GD. After less than 24 hours the affected birds die, the mortality rate is 1% to 60%. The wounds are made of blue-green mangled skin areas, which are not usually feathery, which usually begin with wings and adjoining areas.

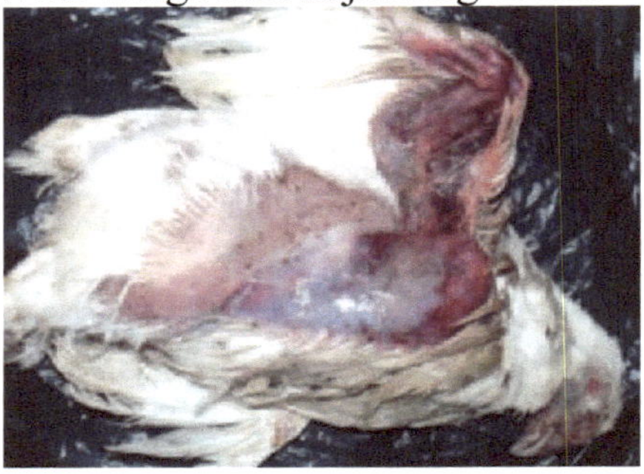

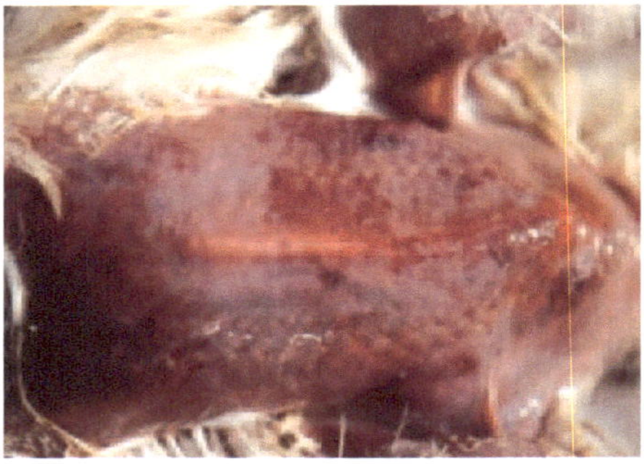

(source of images in diseases,11; MSD animal health)

11. Machinery and equipment

Manual drinker

Automated drinker

Nipple drinker

Nipple pipeline

Manual Feeder Pan

Automated Pan

(source of machinery and equipment images,6; Department of A.H, dairying and Fisheries)

11 Record

Keeping records helps keep track of both physical performance and expenses. It can help keep track of your flock progress. Important for the record is the financial and physical health of a business or operation. Efficient and beneficial poultry work is not guaranteed by keeping a good record, but success without them is impossible without the necessary resources for the management of the record. To maintain a successful flock Maintaining, manufacturing, financially, manufacturing and maintaining healthcare information. Information for a bunch This hand can be done through recording or using computer software. Recording is important.

Records tell an owner or manager, the business / operation has been done and the direction in which it is functioning. Show the strengths and weaknesses of record poultry operations. They provide. Useful information on financial and physical stability for your flock If there is any shortage, the record will show where the changes can be made.

12.1 The registers placed in the breeding farm

1. Attendance and daily wage register.

   This will cover the details of the registered employees, attendance and attendance of them, contract pay is given for labor.
2. Building Register.
   The details of all civil structures in this register, its conservation plan will be spent, and reduce it annually.
3. Equipment Register.
   Feed mill, vehicles, cage, incubator, feeder, water etc. will be registered in this register. Equipment purchase details, repairs done, will be recorded. Annual reduction in equipment and actual post-minus value will be taken to the next year's record.
4. Feed and Feed Endnote Register.
   Some pages can be allocated for each feed agenda. The source of the purchase, the invoice number and date and the cost per unit, can be recorded for each feed content such as opening balance, receipts, issues, loss of storage and closure etc. Comment content about raw quality can also be indicated.

REFERENCES

- Aberra Melesse, 2000. Comparative studies on performance and physiological responses of Ethiopian indigenous ("Angete-melata") chicken and their F1 crosses to long term heat stress. PhD Thesis. Martin-Luther University, Halle-Wittenberg, Berlin.
- Agriculture Skill Council of India
- Agriculture Victoria
- Alemu Yami and Tadelle Dessie, 1997. The Status of Poultry Research and Development. Research Bulletin No. 4. Poultry Commodity Research Program, Debre Zeit Agricultural Research Center, Alemaya University of Agriculture, Ethiopia.
- Amhara National Regional State Bureau of Agriculture and Rural Development (ANRS BoARD), 2006. Poultry Development and Marketing Strategy. Bahir Dar, Ethiopia
- Central Statistical Authority (CSA), 2014. Agricultural Sample Survey Vol. II. Statistical Bulletin No. 331, Addis Ababa, Ethiopia.
- Department of A.H, dairying and Fisheries

- Fisseha M, Abera M, Tadelle D, (2010). Assessment of village chicken production system and evaluation of the productive and reproductive performance local chicken ecotype in Bure district, North West Ethiopia. African Journal of Agricultural Research Vol. 5: 1739-1748.
- Fisseha Moges, Abera Mellesse, and Tadelle Dessie, 2010. Assessment of village chicken production system and evaluation of the productive and reproductive performance of local chicken ecotype in Bure district, North West Ethiopia. African Journal of Agricultural Research Vol. 5(13), 4 July, 2010, 1739-1748pp.
- Halima H., Nesser F.W.C., Van Marle-Koster E., and De Kock A., 2007. Village-based indigenous chicken production system in north-west Ethiopia. Tropical Animal Health and Production. 39:189-197.
- Halima Hassen Mogesse, 2007. Phenotypic and genetic characterization of indigenous chicken populations in North-West Ethiopia. PhD Thesis Submitted to the faculty of natural and agricultural sciences

department of animal, wildlife and grassland Sciences. University of the Free State, Bloemfontein, South Africa.

- http://www.poultryhub.org/health/disease/types-of-disease/
- INDIANA STATE POULTRY ASSOCIATION
- Instructional Materials Service Texas A&M University
- MSD animal health
- Tadelle D., T. Million, Alemu Yami and K.J. Peters, 2003. Village chicken production systems in Ethiopia: Use patterns and performance valuation and chicken products and socio-economic functions of chicken. Livestock Research for Rural Development 15.
- Tadelle Dessie, 1996. Studies on Village Poultry Production Systems in the Central Highlands of Ethiopia. MSc Thesis, Swedish University of Agricultural Sciences.
- ATTRA (Appropriate Technology Transfer for Rural Areas) http://attra.ncat.org/
- The Chicken Health Handbook. Damerow, G. 1994, Storey Books, North Adams, MA. 344 pp.

- Pastured Poultry Profits. Salatin, J. 1993, Polyface, Inc, Swoope, Va. 371 pp. Sources for Chicks
- Phinney Hatchery, 1331 Dell Ave., Walla Walla, WA
- Murray McMurray, Webster City, IA

- Barbut, S. 2002. Poultry Products Processing: An Industry Guide. CRC Press, Boca Raton, Florida, USA.

- Battaglia, R. A. 2001. Handbook of Livestock Management.Prentice Hall, Inc., Upper Saddle River, New Jersey, USA.

- Bebb, D. L. 1990. Mechanized Livestock Feeding. Cambridge University Press, Cambridge, UK.

- Charles, D. R., H. A. Elson, and M. P. Haywood. 1994. Poultry Housing, p. 249-272. In: C. M. Walthes and D. R. Charles (eds.). Livestock Housing. CAB nternational, Wallingford, UK.

- England, T., B. J. Holmes, R. T. Schuler, R. Silha, and R. J. Straub. 2002.

- Precision Land Application of Animal Manure Slurry. ASAE Annual International Meeting / CIGR XVth World Congress, Chicago, Illinois, USA.

- Filmer, D. 2002. Automation is the future for broiler nutrition. World Poultry, 18(6): 33-35.

- Gillespie, J. R. 2002. Modern Livestock and Poultry Production. 6th ed.Thomson Learning, Inc., Columbia, USA.

- Kettlewell, P. J., R. P. Hoxey, and M. A. Mitchell. 2000. Heat Produced by Broiler in a Commercial Transport Vehicle. J. Agric. Engng Res. 75, 315-326.

- Lindley, J.A. and J.H. Whitaker. 1996. Agricultural Buildings and Structures: Poultry Housing, p. 565-590. ASAE, St. Joseph, Michigan, USA.

- Nesheim, M. C., R. E. Austic, and L. E. Card. 1979. Houses and Equipment, p. 146-190. In: Poultry Production. 12th ed. Bailliere Tindall, London, UK.

- Pedersen, S. 1999. Forced Ventilation, p. 68-86. In: E. Bartalie, A. Jongebreur, and D. Moffitt (eds.). CIGR Handbook of Agricultural Engineering: Animal Production and Aquacultural Engineering. ASAE, St. Joseph, Michigan, USA.

- Poultry International: Production, Processing and Marketing Worldwide. 2002. Vol. 41(1): 16-17. Sonsbeck, Germany.

- Puma, M. C., H. Xin, R. S. Gates, and D. J. Burnham. 2001. An Instrumentation System for Studying Feeding and Drinking Behavior of Individual Poultry. Applied Engineering in Agriculture Vol. 17(3): 365-374.
- Tillie, M. 1999. Equipment and Control, p. 115-146. In: E. Bartalie, A.Jongebreur, and D. Moffitt (eds.). CIGR Handbook of Agricultural Engineering: Animal Production and Aquacultural

Engineering. ASAE, St. Joseph, Michigan, USA.

www.ingramcontent.com/pod-product-compliance
Lightning Source LLC
Chambersburg PA
CBHW041528180726
48282CB00052B/105
9789353613174